HEADWORD
ENGLISH
PROGRAMME 3

Chris Culshaw and Jill Dodgson

OXFORD UNIVERSITY PRESS

Contents

Acknowledgements

The authors and publishers would like to thank the following for permission to reproduce copyright material:

Actionaid: letter by Felix Muriki Festo, from letters page, *Going Global* magazine, (No. 2, 1992), Ben Hartshorn (Ed); **Cave Rescue Organization** (Clapham, Lancaster, LA2 8HH): extracts from *Rescue 90*; **Crime Concern/Express Newspapers plc**: poem by Kathryn Bellamy from *YX*; **Innovations Mail Order Ltd** (Telephone 0793 514666) and **Zeon Ltd**: '26-Language Translator', Innovations Catalogue; **Mirror Group Newspapers/Syndication International**: article by Samuel James from *Daily Mirror*; **National Dairy Council**: advertisement; **The National Motor Museum Beaulieu**: car advertisements; **National Westminster Bank plc** and **HMV**: advertisements; **Oxford University Press**: extract from *The Oxford Children's Encyclopedia* (1991), extract from *The New Oxford School Dictionary*, and extracts from W. Shakespeare: *Romeo and Juliet, Oxford School Shakespeare*; **Penguin Group Children's Publishing**: cover Roald Dahl: *Revolting Rhymes*, Puffin Edition; **Random House UK Ltd**: extract from Norman Hunter: *Professor Branestawm's Dictionary*, (Bodley Head), and on behalf of the Estate of Roald Dahl: cover Roald Dahl: *Revolting Rhymes* illustrated by Quentin Blake (first published by Jonathan Cape Ltd); **Reed International Books**: extract from Simon Goodenough: *1500 Fascinating Facts*, (Octopus Books, 1983), and cover Diane Wilmer: *Fireman Sam and the Lost Lamb* (Heinemann), Fireman Sam copyright © 1985 Prism Art & Design Ltd, Fireman Sam illustration copyright © 1988 Reed International Books; **Rover Cars**: advertisement; **Royal Mail**: extracts from leaflets *Post Guide*, and *12 Months of Beautiful British Stamps*, and stamp reproductions; **The Ryvita Company Ltd**: 'Sunblest Cornflakes' packaging; **Scholastic Publications Ltd**: poem by Michael Rosen from *Wouldn't You Like to Know?* (Andre Deutsch Children's Books, an imprint of Scholastic Publications Ltd), © 1977 Michael Rosen; **Solo Syndication**: article from *The Mail on Sunday*, © Mail on Sunday/Solo; **Times Newspapers**: extract from article in Times Educational Supplement; **Today** article from *Today*; **Frederick Warne & Co**: cover Beatrix Potter: *The Tale of Peter Rabbit*, © Frederick Warne & Co, 1902 1987; and **Woolworths plc**: advertisement.

Also **Martin Balmer** and **Joanne Richardson** for their stories, first published here. Thanks are also due to their teacher, **Jennifer Mackness**.

The publishers would like to thank the following for permission to reproduce photographs:

Action Aid p.17; **Mike Dudley** p.18; **John and Eliza Forder** p.48; **National Dairy Council** p.59; **National Motor Museum** p.62; **The Press Association** p.46; **Syndication International** p.14; **The Tullis Collection** pp.41, 43, **Tullis/Diemberger** p.43, **Tullis/Kemp** p.40; **John Walmsley** pp.8, 19.

Although every effort has been made to trace and contact copyright holders before publication this has not been possible in some cases. We apologise for any apparent infringement of copyright and will be pleased to rectify any errors or omissions at the earliest opportunity.

The illustrations are by **Juliet Breese** pp.10, 20, 30, 31, 49; **Tony Chance** pp.16, 21, 37, 38, 50/1, 52/3, 54; **Linda Jeffrey** pp.27, 44, 45; **Pauline Little** pp.11, 56/7; **Jill Newton** p.12; **Judy Stevens** pp.6, 7, 9; **Jacqui Thomas** pp.13, 23, 24, 25; **Marc Vyvyan-Jones** pp.33, 34, 35.

Introduction

Dear Student

Welcome to the **Headwork English Programme**.

Each Students' Book is made up of nine short units. Every unit has a different theme, like holidays, games, food, or ambitions.

We have chosen stories, poems, scripts, photos, and pictures, as well as articles from newspapers and magazines, linked to these themes.

These are followed by **What to do** activities which will help you to develop a wide range of skills in speaking, reading, and writing.

At the start of each unit you will find a **Skills Panel**. This will tell you the main skills you will practise as you work through the unit.

At the end of each unit is a short **Review** which will help you to sum up your progress and talk about any questions you have on particular activities.

We hope you enjoy using **Headwork English Programme**.

Chris Culshaw and Jill Dodgson

Games

SKILLS YOU WILL USE IN THIS UNIT

1 Reading for meaning

2 Writing reviews of simple games

3 Giving and comparing your opinion

4 Writing clear instructions for a simple game

5 Writing a diary entry and a letter

Four Games

Rules

Read through the rules for these 4 games.

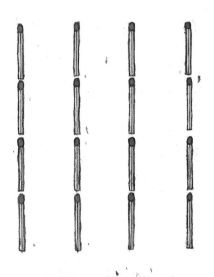

Match trick

This is a game for 2 players.
Set out 16 matches (or paper clips) to make a square as shown here.

Take it in turns to pick up any number of matches. You can pick up from any one row (across) or column (down). But you can only pick up matches that are next to each other. You cannot pick up matches if there is a gap between them.

You win the game when you force your opponent to pick up the last match.

Hopping mad

This is an outdoor game for 2 players.
You play this game on a hard, flat surface.

You stand on one leg and kick a stone (with the same foot) across a line.

The winner is the person who reaches the line 25 metres away first.

Tearaway

This is a game for 2 or more players. You will need lots of old newspaper. One player is blindfolded and given a sheet of newspaper. This player has to tear out the shape of a person.

Each player takes a turn. The one who tears out the best shape wins.

(This is quite a hard game! You can start off with easy shapes – a circle, square, or triangle – before you try harder ones.)

Bluff

This is a game for 3 or more players. Each player needs 3 small objects (e.g. marbles, coins, buttons).

The players stand in a circle, facing each other. They put their hands behind their backs and put some or all of the objects into one hand. On the count of three all players hold out the closed fist with the hidden objects.

Then each player takes a turn at guessing the total number of objects hidden in the fists. Each guess must be different.

You win if you guess the correct total, or if your guess is nearest.

You each have 3 lives.

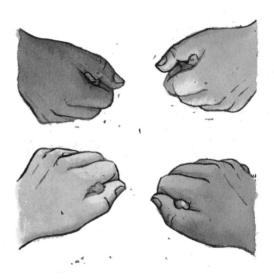

What to do

In a small group

Play these games and write a review of each one like this:

Match trick
We liked/disliked this game because...
This game is suitable for... year olds.
We would give this game a score of... out of 10 because...

What Makes a Good Game?

A Terry

I like games like chess. They make you think. Most games for kids are a waste of time.

B Claire

I like really silly games. Crazy games that make you laugh. Games you play just for fun. I don't care about winning.

C Latha

I like ball games like football. I don't like board-games. They are boring. I like plenty of action.

D Tom

I like games where all the family can join in. The more players the better. We have a great time at Christmas playing cards and dominoes, games like that.

What to do

On your own

Write a sentence like this about each person above:

> A I agree/disagree with Terry because…

What to do next

On your own

1 Look back to the 4 games on pages 6–7.
   Which of these games do you think these 4 people would like best?
   Write a sentence about each person like this:
   > A I think Terry would like… because…
2 Make a list of 4 or 5 other games that you think one of the 4 people above would like.

Which Game?

A A board-game for 2 or more players. You throw a dice to see how far to move. You start at the bottom of the board and try to get to the top. If you land on certain squares, you have to move backwards. You race ahead if you land on others.

B This is a board-game for 2 to 6 players. It is not suitable for very young children. If you like puzzles you will like this game, because you have to work out whodunnit.

C A board-game for 2 or more players. Each game can last a very long time. There are a lot of rules. This is not really suitable for children under 8. You have to make as much money as you can. You do this by buying land, houses, and hotels.

D This is a board-game. It is one of the most popular games in the world. It is a game for 2 or more players. Each player has 7 tiles. You have to place the tiles on the board to make words and score points.

E This is a board-game for 2 or more players. It is not suitable for young children. If you have a good memory you will be good at this game. You have to answer questions on sport, history, science, and many other subjects.

Game names

1 Scrabble	**3** Cluedo	**5** Snakes and Ladders
2 Monopoly	**4** Trivial Pursuit	

What to do

In pairs

Match the description of each game, A–E, to its name, 1–5.

What to do next

On your own

You are a designer for a games company. Pick one of these games (or a game you know well) and design a new package for it. Think about the age and number of players and what will make the game attractive to them.

Hangman

This is a pencil and ....1....... game for two players. Player **A** thinks of a word. Player **B** has to ....2....... this 'mystery' word. This is how the ....3....... is played.

Player **A** tells Player **B** how many ....4....... are in the mystery word. **A** draws a line like this:

— — — — — — — —

Each dash ....5....... for a letter. (This mystery word has eight letters.)

Then **B** tries to guess what these letters are. If **B** makes a correct ....6....... **A** puts that letter in. If **B** makes a ....7....... guess **A** draws the first part of the gallows.

Every time **B** makes a wrong guess **A** adds another bit of the ....8....... .

The gallows look like this:

Next, **A** starts to draw a person hanging from the gallows. Every time **B** makes a wrong guess **A** adds a bit of the person. **A** draws the ....9......., then the body, then the arms (one at a time) and lastly the legs.

If **B** has not ....10....... the word by now they are 'hanged' and **A** has won.

To make the game ....11....... **A** can give **B** a clue, such as 'I am thinking of a seven letter word. It is the ....12....... of a town near here'. Or 'The word is the name of an animal'.

What to do

In pairs
Fill in the words missing from these instructions. Write your answers like this: 1 = *paper*

What to do next

On your own
Write a description of how to play another simple game, e.g. Noughts and Crosses. It may help to use diagrams or cartoons.

A Weekend with the Players

What to do

In pairs

Make a list of all the games you can spot in the illustration.

What to do next

On your own

You are friendly with Alison Player. Her family invites you to stay for the weekend. Friday night starts with a gentle game of Snakes and Ladders. But soon things get very hectic!

1 Write your diary entries for Saturday and Sunday, describing what actually happens and how you feel about it.
2 Write a thank you letter to the Players.
   Remember, be tactful, you do not want to hurt your friends' feelings.

END OF UNIT REVIEW
1
2

Look At It This Way

SKILLS YOU WILL USE IN THIS UNIT

1 Thinking about different points of view
2 Writing a pattern poem
3 Writing a humorous letter
4 Reading for information
5 Writing to give information

Song of a Bear

There is danger where I move my feet.
I am a whirlwind. There is danger where
    I move my feet.
I am a grey bear.
When I walk, where I step lightning
    flies from me.
Where I walk, one to be feared.
Where I walk, long life.
One to be feared I am.
There is danger where I walk.

Navajo (North American Indian)

What to do

On your own

Song of a Bear is a poem about how a bear sees itself. Write a poem in the same style about another dangerous wild animal, such as an eagle, snake, shark or tiger.

For example, if you choose an eagle, you might begin:

There is danger where my shadow falls…

Problems Page

Dear Maureen,
I am a lamp-post.
Every Saturday evening at five o'clock
three boys wearing blue and white scarves
blue and white hats
waving their arms in the air
and shouting,
come my way.
Sometimes they kick me.
Sometimes they kiss me.
What should I do
to get them to make up their minds?
Yours bewilderedly,

Annie Onlight.

Michael Rosen

What to do

On your own

1 In the poem, *Problems Page*, we see the world through the eyes of a lamp-post.
   Write the answer that Maureen, the Agony Aunt, might have sent to Annie Onlight.
2 Think of another object that might feel like writing to Maureen about a problem. Write the letter.
   e.g. Dear Maureen, I am a washing machine. I don't know which way to turn next. I feel washed out all the time... .
   Ask a partner to write Maureen's reply.

A

Snappy burglars leave behind a photo

SCHOOLBOY burglars left a souvenir of their raid on granny Joan Denbigh's home ... a photo of one of the pint-sized crooks snapped by his mate.

It turned up when 68 year-old Joan sent the film from her camera to be developed. There among the family holiday snaps was a clear colour photo of one of the tear-aways who stole a TV set, two video recorders, a micro-wave oven and other valuables worth £2,300.

But they forgot to pocket the £45 Olympus.

And the candid camera put them on the spot – just like a clip from Jeremy Beadle's 'You've Been Framed' television show.

Joan, of Armley Ridge Road, Leeds, said yesterday: 'The youngster only looks 10 or 12.

He's standing in my kitchen wearing leather gloves and looking very furtive.'

Joan's Husband, Joshua, 76, said, 'He looks as if butter wouldn't melt in his mouth.'

Police have already caught the culprits so the snap won't be needed to help track them down.

Joan said: 'I might pin it up and throw darts at it – that's how angry I still feel about it.'

Daily Mirror 20 Feb 1993

B

I've been framed... tiny burglar caught on film

A COUPLE got more than they bargained for when their holiday snaps came back from the developers.

For among Joan and Joshua Denbigh's photos was the face of a teeny burglar who was part of a gang who ransacked their home. The boy, whose face is obscured for legal reasons, was snapped by a pal as they stole a TV, two video recorders and microwave worth £2,300.

But the bungling burglars forgot to stash the camera with the rest of their haul.

'When we leafed through the pictures we got the shock of our lives,' said Joan.

The couple's Leeds home was raided in July 1991 but they did not develop the film until this week.

Joan, 68, added: 'The lad looks angelic. He's standing in my kitchen wearing leather gloves and looking very furtive.'

The young gang, aged between 10 and 12, were caught by police in January last year and dealt with at juvenile court.

Today 20 Feb 1993

What to do

In a small group

1 Pick out 3 facts that appear in stories A and B.
2 Find 2 facts that appear in B, but not in A.
3 Both stories treat the crime in a 'jokey' way,
   e.g. A describes the criminals as 'pint-sized crooks' and
   B describes them as 'teeny burglars'.
   Find other words or phrases that suggest the reporters are trying to write a light-hearted account of the crime.
4 How do you think Mr and Mrs Denbigh felt about these two reports?
5 How do you think the criminals felt about them?
6 What do you think about the way the crime is reported?

What to do next

In a small group

Pick out the most important details of the crime. Your notes from questions 1 and 2 above will help you with this.

Use them to write a news item to be included in a local TV news bulletin. This news item must not exceed 30 seconds!

Choose one person to read your news item. Rehearse it and then time the reading.

Me

I used to think it was great fun
Watching them pick on her
Being so bitchy
It must have really hurt
It used to be quite funny
Until I looked to see
That it wasn't her they were picking on
But this time it was me
I wished I hadn't laughed now
Because it aches inside
The trouble that they caused me
Was far too much to hide
Now I know what it feels like
Being picked on time after time
I now know not to laugh at them
And that bullying is a crime

Kathryn Bellamy

What to do

In pairs

1 What did the writer think was 'great fun'?
2 Why does she suddenly see things differently?
3 She says 'bullying is a crime'. Do you agree?
4 How do you think bullies would describe what they do
  e.g. fun, a good laugh?
5 What makes somebody become a bully?
6 Does this poem have a moral? If so, try to write a sentence
  that sums it up.

What to do next

On your own

If bullying is a crime what kinds of punishment should bullies
receive? Make two lists of punishments (one serious, one
humorous) for various types of bullying. Set them out in a
chart like this:

Offence	Serious punishment	Humorous punishment
Name calling	School detention	1 day in school stocks

Money, Money

We get pocket money from our parents, sometimes 10-20 Kenyan shillings [50Ks = £1]. Not all children get it, some of their parents are very poor, they cannot afford it.

We can use it to buy biros, pencils, and books for school, and ice cream, sweets, cakes, and sodas. If I was given 1 million Ks I could buy plots of land to grow maize, beans, coffee, and tea. I could also buy clothes and pay school fees. A Mercedes Benz is a top car to buy. Government Ministers drive Mercedes in Kenya. If school is closed we try our best to do business, like selling sukumawiki (greens). A sack costs 60Ks and we sell it for 80Ks. I keep the money and pay for school fees. There is never enough. I could keep money for the future, such as when I have visitors. I could also save some.

Felix Muriki Festo, aged 16
Baba Dogo School, Kariobangi, Kenya

from Action Aid's magazine, *Going Global*

What to do

In a small group

1 Discuss what you spend your pocket money on.
   Work out the price in Kenyan shillings of the things you buy.
2 If someone gave you £1 million, what would you do with it?
3 How can young people your age earn money?

What to do next

On your own

Write a letter to Felix giving him your views on earning, saving, and spending money. Use sentences like the ones Felix uses:

   e.g. *We can use it to buy…*
        If I was given £1 million…

Felix may not know very much about your country. It may help him to compare his life-style with yours if you tell him how much some things you buy would cost in Kenyan shillings.

END OF UNIT REVIEW

1
2

Unit 3

Early Learning

SKILLS YOU WILL LEARN IN THIS UNIT

1 Giving views on children's stories
2 Discussing children's writing
3 Reading stories written by young children
4 Writing a story for young children
5 Drafting a story with a partner

Children's Stories

What to do

In a small group

1 Discuss your memories of reading, writing, and listening to stories at Primary School. Give reasons for what you say.
   ● Which story do you remember best?
   ● Was there anything you really disliked reading?
   ● What did you like writing about?
2 List the most popular and unpopular things about reading and writing mentioned by your group.

What to do next

In groups

1 When young children are writing stories they are helped by different things. Put points A–F in order of importance:
   A writing stories with pictures in them
   B writing about subjects that interest them
   C writing lots of different stories
   D writing about themselves
   E being given extra words to go with the subject
   F talking with a teacher

Writing for Children

> ...and as you look up to the sky, you see a parachute floating down. From it is dangling a key.

Martin's story

Martin, who is 5, wrote this story about the parachute and the key.

I w t t w v my mummy and

I went to the woods with my Mummy and

daddy and we f d a c y

Daddy and we found a key

and wey t c it hom

and we took it home.

What to do

In a small group

Imagine you are Martin's teacher. Write a comment on his story writing. Comment on:
- 2 or 3 things Martin has achieved
- 2 or 3 things it would be useful for him to learn

Think about the way he has spelt certain words, the letters he has missed out, and the punctuation he has used.

Joanne's story

Joanne, who is 6, wrote a longer story about the parachute and the key.

One day I was walking
through a wood with Callie and
I saw a key on a parachute.
We wondered where it leads to.
I found a box. I saw if the
key fitted it did, I opened it
up and there was a family of mice,
I took the mice home and kept
them as pets.

One day I was wurking
thow a wud with callie and
I saw a kee on a parshot.
We wunder were it leds to.
I fond a box, I sed if the
kee fitd it did, I opnd it
up and thay was a famle of misse,
I tuc the miese hom and cept
them as a pets.

What to do

On your own
Use Joanne's words and the picture story on page 21 to help you write a simple story which a 6 or 7 year old would enjoy. Call your story 'The Key from the Sky'.

Tips for writing a children's story.

1. Write a paragraph for each picture.
2. Make the most of the ideas Joanne enjoys, e.g. being with her friend, a touch of mystery and suspense, finding little animals to look after.
3. Find simple but interesting words to describe important things like the key and the mice.
4. Include one thing Joanne might think or feel during each stage of the story.
5. List any words which may be new to the reader.

In pairs

1 Swap your work with your partner. Comment on each other's stories and discuss possible changes.
2 Word-process the final version of your story.
3 Share your story with a 6 or 7 year old, if possible.

END OF UNIT REVIEW

1
2

Unit 4

Get The Message

SKILLS YOU WILL USE IN THIS UNIT

1 Reading a short story
2 Discussing and giving opinions
3 Reading a leaflet for information
4 Gathering and presenting information
5 Using reference books and leaflets for research

So Near and Yet So Far

Adam was crazy about Vanda, a girl in his class. Vanda lived in the next street and her garden backed on to Adam's garden. Adam could see Vanda's bedroom from his bedroom window. Vanda used to sit at her window, doing her homework, and so did Adam. Night after night they would sit, the two small gardens between them. So near… and yet so far.

For weeks Adam had tried to pluck up the courage to ask Vanda out. But he was very shy, and Vanda was always with a crowd of girls. At last he made up his mind to 'phone and ask her out. He wanted to take her to the Bonfire Night disco the following week.

He went to the 'phone box at the corner, by the post office. If he rang her from home his brother was bound to listen in. Of course the 'phone was out of order as usual. Some idiot had jammed a foreign coin in one of the slots.

He went home and decided to write a letter. He thought about asking his mother for a stamp. But that would have meant awkward questions, like: 'Good grief Adam, you haven't been writing letters, have you? The last time you wrote a letter was when you were five when you wrote to Santa, asking for a… .' No, he did not want his mother quizzing him.

He ran back to the post office just in time to see 'Open'

turn to 'Closed'. The stamp machine on the wall outside the shop was empty, so he went to the off-licence round the corner.

When he got back to the postbox Terry Hands and a gang of his nasty mates were hanging around. Terry had a pocketful of fireworks. He pulled out a rip-rap and lit it. He shouted at Adam, 'Clear off… or I'll stick this down your trousers!' Adam ran off down the street… forgetting to post the letter.

The next day Adam planned to go to the postbox on his way to school. There was a policewoman standing outside the shop. She called him over. 'Do you know anything about this?' she said, pointing to the postbox. Smoke was coming from the letter slot.

'No,' Adam said and walked on, the letter still in his pocket. That night Adam had a very strange dream. He had tied his letter to Vanda (still unposted!) onto the leg of a homing pigeon. He had opened his bedroom window and released the bird, when a huge eagle dropped down out of the night sky and carried the poor pigeon away.

Then Adam was standing on the roof of the house waving two pairs of bright red boxer shorts, like semaphore flags, still desperate to get a message to Vanda. Suddenly, he felt himself falling and falling as the roof of the house became a huge sheet of paper. On this sheet of paper, in letters a mile high, was the message: 'Vanda, will you go out with me?' The paper folded itself into a giant paper plane, which carried Adam over the gardens towards Vanda's house.

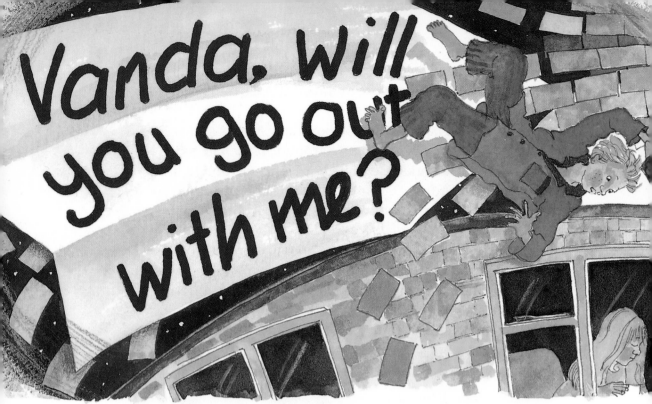

Vanda, will you go out with me?

Just as he was about to crash through her bedroom window Adam was woken by his mother tugging at his toe.

'Adam, wake up! 'Phone. For you.' His mother dropped the cordless 'phone on to the bed.

Adam muttered from under the duvet. 'What time is it? Am I late for school?'

'It's Saturday. And it's 10 o'clock. You look dreadful. You should get to bed earlier.'

Adam yawned. 'I was dreaming… .' He picked up the 'phone. 'Hello, who is it?'

'Guess,' said a girl's voice.

'Who is this?' he said crossly, still half asleep.

'Can't you guess?'

'You sound like my cousin Rita, but she's in Canada.'

'I'm not that far away. Look out of the window.'

Adam crawled out of bed and opened the curtains. There at her window, across the gardens, stood Vanda, 'phone in hand. She waved.

'Oh,' said Adam suddenly wide awake, 'It's you. What do you want?'

There was a long silence. Then Vanda said, 'Are you going to the Bonfire Night disco…?'

What to do

On your own

Draw some simple cartoons to show the various ways Adam tries to get in touch with Vanda.

What to do next

In a small group

1 Discuss how these things might have helped Adam solve his problem.

2 Can you think of enough different ways of communicating to make up a 'Communications Alphabet'?
Each item in the alphabet has to be a way of sending messages.

    e.g. **A** is for Airmail   **B** is for Balloon

You could also include some more creative ways of communicating:

    e.g. **P** is for Pea-shooter!

When you have agreed on a group alphabet copy it out and choose 8 to 10 letters to illustrate.

What to do next

On your own

When Vanda and Adam meet at the disco they still have a 'communication problem'. Vanda is relaxed and chatty, but Adam is very shy. Write 10 to 12 lines of a playscript to show the differences between them. It might start like this:

    Vanda: Hi Adam, great disco, isn't it? Glad you came?
    Adam: Yeh... sure... right.

Post It!

Read these extracts from a *Post Guide* by the Royal Mail.

YOUR LOCAL POSTCODES

Postcodes make it possible to sort letters much faster, using automation. So using the Postcode is one of the most important ways you can help us give you a faster service.

The Postcode idea is very simple. Each part of your code identifies a more and more local area, right down to 15 or so individual addresses. Many buildings – blocks of flats for example – have their own unique Postcode. The country's 24 million 1.6 million Postcodes cover the country's 24 million letterboxes.

This tells us which one of our 120 Postcode Areas the letter goes to.

The Sector within the District.

LS 30 1 AA

These two characters pinpoint the address to within 15 letterboxes on average!

Within the Area, which Postcode District.

THE ONES WE CAN'T DELIVER

Every week we get around 2 million letters nationally which are impossible to deliver. Some people have moved. Some addresses may be incorrect – or illegible. We even see some envelopes correctly stamped, but without one word of an address!

Unless there is a return address on the envelope, we must open your mail to look for your address so that we can send your letter back to you. This takes time.

REMEMBER THE RETURN ADDRESS

It's easy to avoid all this. Just write your own address on the back of the envelope. Then, if for any reason we cannot deliver your letter, we can simply send it back to you – unopened and without delay.

BLOCK CAPITALS PLEASE!

It makes it easier – and quicker – for us to sort your mail if you write the **POSTTOWN** in capitals as shown in the picture and put in the Postcode!

SENDING LETTERS ABROAD

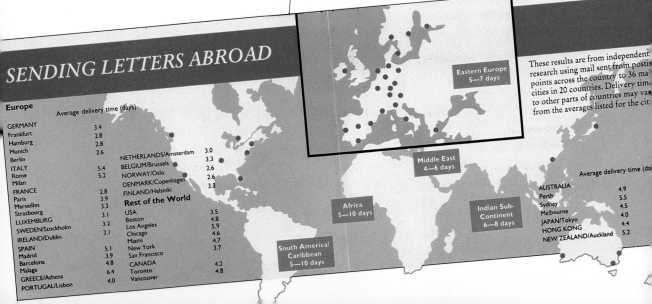

These results are from independent research using mail sent from posting points across the country to 36 major cities in 20 countries. Delivery times to other parts of countries may vary from the averages listed for the cities

Eastern Europe 5–7 days

Middle East 4–6 days

Africa 5–10 days

Indian Sub-Continent 6–8 days

South America/Caribbean 5–10 days

Europe	Average delivery time (days)
GERMANY	
Frankfurt	3.4
Hamburg	2.8
Munich	2.8
Berlin	2.6
ITALY	
Rome	5.4
Milan	5.2
FRANCE	
Paris	2.8
Marseilles	3.9
Strasbourg	3.3
LUXEMBURG	3.1
SWEDEN/Stockholm	3.2
IRELAND/Dublin	3.1
SPAIN	
Madrid	5.1
Barcelona	3.9
Malaga	4.8
GREECE/Athens	6.4
PORTUGAL/Lisbon	4.0

	Average delivery time (days)
NETHERLANDS/Amsterdam	3.0
BELGIUM/Brussels	3.3
NORWAY/Oslo	2.6
DENMARK/Copenhagen	2.6
FINLAND/Helsinki	3.3
Rest of the World	
USA	
Boston	3.5
Los Angeles	4.8
Chicago	5.9
Miami	4.6
New York	4.7
San Francisco	3.7
CANADA	
Toronto	4.2
Vancouver	4.8

	Average delivery time (days)
AUSTRALIA	
Perth	4.9
Sydney	5.5
Melbourne	4.5
JAPAN/Tokyo	4.0
HONG KONG	4.4
NEW ZEALAND/Auckland	5.2

In pairs

1 How many postcodes are needed for the whole country?

2 Do Tom and Santi live in the same street? Give a reason for your answer.

Our postcodes are nearly the same. Mine is OX3 7JB....

... and mine is OX3 8JB.

3 Ask as many people as you can to tell you their postcode.
Make a 'postcode map' of your local area.
See if you can mark some postal districts and sectors on it.

4 How many letters each year does the Royal Mail have problems delivering?

5 Why are some letters impossible to deliver?

6 What happens to a letter that cannot be delivered? What can the sender do to help this?

7 If you were on holiday in these places and sent postcards home, how long would they take?
  ● Near Malaga in Spain   ● Paris
  ● Disneyland near Miami   ● Rome

8 An uncle in Australia has sent one of you a birthday present. You want to thank him. Between you find out:
  ● the cost of sending a postcard to Australia (first class)
  ● the cost of 'phoning Australia (3 minute call at cheap rate)
Write 2 sentences about the difference in price and what you would decide to do.

What to do next

In a small group

You will need a large outline map of the world.

Ask as many people as you can which foreign countries they get letters and cards from. Mark these on your outline map.

Show clearly the name of the country and the name of the person who gets mail from that country.

If possible collect some stamps from these countries and add these to your map.

Say It With a Stamp

Look carefully at these special issue stamps from the Royal Mail.

Barcelona
Paralympics,
1992

Protection
of the
Environment

Dinosaurs:
Tyrannosaurus

The English
Civil War:
350th
Anniversary

Tennyson: Centenary
of Death

RSPCA: 150th Anniversary

On your own

Write 3 or 4 sentences about 4 of the stamps. Say why you think the Royal Mail chose each subject for these stamps.

Find out 2 facts about each subject. (A good junior encyclopedia will help with this.)

Give your opinion of the design of each stamp. Set out your answers like this:

> This stamp shows a dinosaur. The Royal Mail probably chose dinosaurs for its stamps because...
> I found out that dinosaurs...
> I like/dislike the design of this stamp because...

Future communication: fax facts

Modern technology is providing an electronic way to send letters and documents. Electronic mail (E mail) systems send information from one computer to another either by cable or by telephone link. Fax (facsimile) machines code information so that it can be sent along telephone lines and decoded at the receiving fax.

Individuals and companies may have their own equipment. In some countries, the official post office and courier companies offer E-mail and fax services to help people send messages more quickly.

Oxford Children's Encyclopedia

What to do

In pairs

1 Make a list of jobs that might disappear or change if everyone started using E-mail instead of letter post.
2 Think of other ways that people might use to send messages in the future. Illustrate them with cartoons.

END OF UNIT REVIEW

1
2

Word Worlds

Language Soup

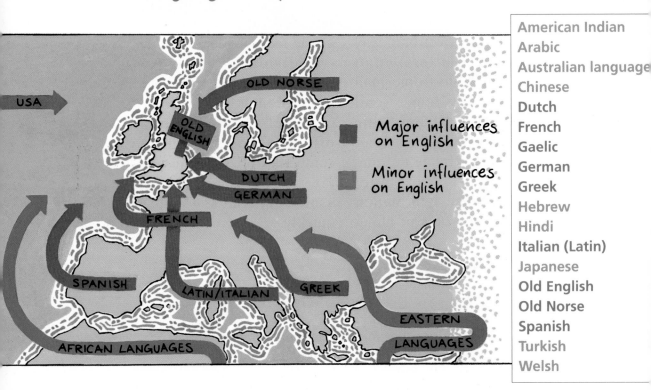

American Indian
Arabic
Australian language
Chinese
Dutch
French
Gaelic
German
Greek
Hebrew
Hindi
Italian (Latin)
Japanese
Old English
Old Norse
Spanish
Turkish
Welsh

English is like a soup of words and phrases from many other languages. In the past these words have been brought over by settlers and invading armies. Today they come through TV, pop music, and newspapers. New products, e.g. the personal stereo, also create new words like 'walkman'.

The study of the origin of words is called **etymology**. These entries from a school dictionary tell you the meaning of each word and give information about its origins (shown by the highlighter).

rucksack *noun* a bag on straps for carrying on the back.
from German *rücken* = back, + *sack*

mother *verb* look after someone in a motherly way.
from Old English *modor*

New Oxford School Dictionary

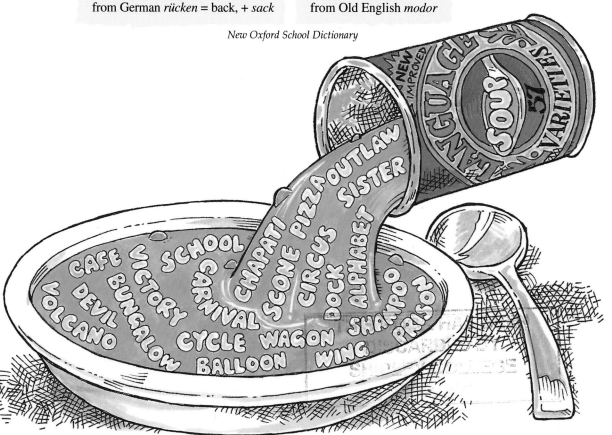

What to do

In pairs

1 Find out the origins of the words in the soup above, using etymological dictionaries. Make a chart like this to record your findings:

Word	Origin
Cycle	Greek *kyklos* = circle

2 Look through the dictionary and note down any words that have the same root languages as the ones in your chart.

Amazing 26-language translator

Most translators only offer you a limited choice of languages – now you'll never be lost for words in an amazing total of 26 different languages. This versatile databank translates English into 1000 words in each language, yet measures a slim credit-card size, 5.5 cm x 9.0 cm x 0.5 cm to fit easily in a pocket. Features include 2-line, 12 character LCD screen and full word scrolling. Powered by CR2025 battery (supplied).

26-Language Translator
£39.95   QQ849A

What to do

In a small group

1 Discuss what this machine does.
2 What kind of people might use it? In what sort of situations? Jot down your ideas about this.
3 How many words does the translator store?
4 There are hundreds of languages spoken around the world. How did the makers decide which languages to build into the machine?
5 How did the makers choose which English words to translate? Give reasons.
   Some words have special importance in all languages, e.g. police, danger, stop, taxi, hotel. What other words would it be useful to include?

What to do next

On your own

You buy a language translator and take it on holiday, but accidentally drop it in the hotel swimming pool. When you try to use it again things go badly wrong!
   Write a postcard to your best friend explaining what happens when you use the faulty translator.

Why Do We Say...?

Why are hitch-hikers called hitch-hikers?

Hitch-hiking gets its name from the way two people used to ride with one horse in America about a hundred years ago. If two travellers had to get from New York to Boston, say, but only had one horse this is how they did it.
The first traveller would ride ahead to an agreed place. Then he would tie (hitch) the horse to a tree and start to walk (hike).

Meanwhile, the second traveller who had started the journey on foot, walked until he came to the horse. He would then ride the next stage of the journey. He too would hitch the horse at an agreed place and carry on hiking. This way both travellers hitched and hiked their way across country. It was a good idea... unless someone stole the horse while both travellers were hiking!

Simon Goodenough (adapted from *15 000 Fascinating Facts*)

What to do

On your own

Draw a series of simple pictures (like a comic strip) to show the origin of the term 'hitch-hiking'.
Label the drawings clearly, so that someone who had not read the explanation above would understand how the term originated.

What to do next

On your own

Choose one of these phrases and write 4 or 5 sentences to explain how it might have originated. Be creative!
- raining cats and dogs
- give someone the sack
- over the moon
- sleep like a log
- pull someone's leg
- mad as a hatter

Try to find out the real origin of the phrase.

Daft Dictionary Definitions

buoyant	copper nitrate	fungi	hyacinth	khaki
male insect	what policemen get paid for working in the evenings	a comedian	friendly greeting for Cynthia	thing for starting a motor car

Norman Hunter (from *Professor Branestawm's Dictionary*)

What to do

In a small group

1 Each of these definitions is a play on words, e.g. buoyant sounds like 'boy ant' – a male insect.
   Find the word play in the other definitions.
2 Use a dictionary to find the real meanings of the 5 words.

What to do next

On your own

Try making up your own daft definitions. Think of words that split into two or more parts. Words about 8 to 12 letters long are easier to split than shorter ones.
   Start by making up definitions for these words, then try to write 3 or 4 of your own.

● cartoon   (hint: car/tune)
● somersault   (hint: summer/salt)
● trapeze   (hint: trap/ease)

On the Move

Imagine a creature called a 'wug'. Now imagine a very small one. What would you call it?

'A wuglet', say most people over 30, according to a recent survey. But the same survey also shows that children aged between 11 and 14 are more likely to go for 'mini-wug' or even 'microwug'.

The English language is constantly on the move, and one thing which is changing, it seems, is the way in which we form new words.

(from *Times Educational Supplement* 5 June 1992)

What to do

In a small group

1 The English language is 'constantly on the move'. Discuss which of these statements best sums up why. Give reasons for your choice.

A People get bored using the same words all the time, so they invent new ones.

B New words are brought over from other countries and replace old ones.

C We need new words to describe new situations and objects.

D You have fashions in words, just like you have fashions in clothes or music. Old words go out of fashion and new ones take their place.

2 Which of these words do you think have been added to the English language since 1900? Give reasons.

- television
- telescope
- mechanic
- lipstick
- calculate
- lager
- triangle
- teenager
- police
- lightning
- farmer
- polystyrene

END OF UNIT REVIEW

1

2

Unit 6

Ambitions

> **SKILLS YOU WILL USE IN THIS UNIT**
>
> 1 Reading biographies and comparing lives
> 2 Thinking about paragraphs
> 3 Discussing opinions
> 4 Writing and reading a radio announcement
> 6 Writing part of an autobiography

King of the Matadors

Corridas

Bullfights or 'corridas' have gone on in Spain for hundreds of years. There is some opposition to bullfighting but it is generally very popular. Bullfights, like football, are shown on television. The biggest bull ring in Madrid holds 23,000 spectators.

Bullfighting is seen as an art rather than a sport. Many people admire the skilled moves of a bullfighter or 'matador' in the same way as they might admire the steps of a dancer.

What to do

On your own

A **biography** is the story of someone's life told by another person.

Read this short biography of the Spanish bullfighter, Manolete, and the account of his career which follows on page 37.

The story of a matador

Manolete was, for a time, the most popular bullfighter in Spain. He had made millions before he was thirty. Two days before he was going to retire he fought a bull called Islero. He and the bull killed each other. The whole country mourned when Manolete died at Linares in 1947.

Manolete's last fight

Manolete battled against his fear because he wanted people to think he was the best. At first people used to laugh at him because of his strange looks and clumsiness. But the people never laughed at the way he killed bulls. Manolete used to throw himself over the bull's lowered head, within centimetres of the deadly horns and sink his sword between the shoulders. 'He's going to get killed that way some day,' said the experts.

Manolete said: 'My knees start to quake when I first see my name on the posters and they don't stop until the end of the season.'

With the help of a clever manager Manolete became better and better at his art. His cape became a live thing in his hands as he teased the bull closer and closer to his body. The people loved it. By 1939 he was in the big league, fighting only the fiercer, older bulls. He rose to fame – every fight and every season was better than the one before. By 1946 when he toured Mexico the crowds welcomed him as 'the King of Matadors'.

When he returned to Spain he found he was no longer the hero of the people. It was time to retire but Manolete needed to prove he was still the best. He would fight one more season. The crowds turned against their one-time hero. No matter how daring Manolete was they always cheered the other matadors louder.

On 28 August 1947 Manolete faced the bull called Islero at
Linares. Islero was one of the fierce Miura breed, which
are known as 'the bulls of death'. Islero was even more
dangerous as it often hooked its horns to the right and a
matador must go over the right horn to kill. Manolete began
by giving one of his most death-defying performances. He
drew Islero closer and closer and the crowd went wild with
excitement.

'They keep demanding more and more of me in every fight and
I have no more to give.'

The climax came when he looked to the stands as the bull
thundered past him. Manolete would not spoil this
performance for anything. He ignored all the dangers as he
hurled himself over Islero's right horn. As Manolete thrust
his sword Islero twisted his horn to the right and drove it
into the man's groin. Manolete tried to fight the horn out of
his body before he was thrown to the sand. Islero then
spiked at him twice, staggered, choked, and fell over dead.
    Manolete came round briefly to ask whether the bull had
died. Even on the operating table he wanted to know

whether he had pleased the crowd. They had given Manolete both the ears and the tail of the dead bull, the highest honour a crowd can give a matador. He had given them his life.

What to do

In a small group

1 Discuss your views about bullfighting. Talk about why you think it might be so important to Spanish people.
2 Decide which of these ideas comes in each paragraph of 'Manolete's last fight'. Write your conclusions like this:

Paragraph 1 = D

A On 28 August 1947 Manolete chose to fight a very dangerous bull.
B Manolete did not like it when the Spanish crowds did not look up to him anymore.
C Even as he was dying Manolete wanted to know what the people thought of him.
D The way Manolete killed bulls was by throwing himself over the horns.
E Islero and Manolete gave each other fatal wounds.
F Manolete rose to fame and increased his skill as a fighter.

What to do next

On your own

1 Write a sentence giving your opinion about each of the statements below. Say whether you think A, B, or C is the most likely reason for Manolete's death.
   A The bull, Islero, was a particularly bad one and Manolete allowed his fear to get the better of him.
   B The crowds wanted too much from Manolete and he was too proud for his own safety.
   C Manolete took part in this bullfight because he wanted to earn even more money.
2 Write a radio announcement telling of Manolete's death. Include:
   ● facts of his death
   ● details about his life
   ● people's views on bullfighting.
   Practise reading your announcement and then record it on cassette.

Climbing the Peaks

Julie Tullis' story

'I have gone to practise karate when I have felt so tired that all I've wanted to do is go to bed. But once you are on the mat, you forget about it and carry on, for two hours perhaps, until it's over. It's the same with mountaineering. Once you are committed to a mountain you can only go up... It's heartbreaking to go down.' (1)

Julie Tullis, 1939-86, was a woman of great strength. She was a black belt, second Dan, in Karate and Aikido and during her middle age rose to become one of the country's finest mountaineers. In 1985 she was the first British woman to be part of an expedition to the world's highest mountain, Everest. She spent an incredible 52 days of that year living above 20,000 feet.

In 1986 Julie made her third trip to K2, the world's second

highest mountain. Her greatest ambition was to reach its summit. A few weeks before she left, she seemed to have doubts about achieving this ambition. In a letter she wrote about all the people who had died on K2, 'I have buried so many good friends, and so many good climbers have died, that I have little heart left to climb my mountain of mountains'. (2) But Julie had to go back to K2. It was as if the mountain held a fatal fascination for her.

Julie reached the summit of her dream mountain on the evening of 4 August 1986. Julie and her companion both fell as they started to come down. The two saved each other from injury but were so shaken and tired that they spent the night in a hole dug in the snow. They reached camp '4' (26,500 ft) at noon the next day, but by evening they were trapped in a furious blizzard.

The storm was to last five days. The temperature fell to minus 30°C and the wind rose to over 100 kph. The climbers did not have much food or fuel because of the difficulties of carrying it. During the night of the seventh Julie died as she slept. Only two of the six people trapped in camp '4' escaped from the mountain.

'A ticket to K2!' Julie had joked at a railway station in Stoke-on-Trent. 'Single or return?' the ticket clerk replied. (3) There

was no return. Her passion for K2 drove her to its summit. 'Even though I know that the odds of injury and survival must be shortening, I have to go back. One in twelve Himalayan mountaineers die for their ruling passion. But life is short and there has to be a reason to live beyond purely survival... If I could choose a place to die it would be in the mountains.' (4)

1 Interview with Julie Tullis, 1985
2 Letter from Julie Tullis, 1986
3 Conversation with Julie Tullis, 1986
4 From Julie Tullis' autobiography, *Clouds from Both Sides*, 1986

What to do

In pairs

1 Check the meaning of any of the words in this word bank which you are unsure of.
2 List the words or phrases which could describe Julie Tullis.
3 Put a star by any of these which could also describe Manolete.
4 Write 2 or 3 sentences which describe the main differences between Julie Tullis and Manolete.

ambitious	skilful	strong	admirable
wanting	self-fulfilled	tragic	sympathetic
heroic	persevering	rich	passionate
determined	competitive	reckless	impressive
humorous	popular	unlucky	self-controlled
committed	wanting fame	self-reliant	aware of dangers

What to do next

In a small group

1 Discuss the footnotes (points 1–4) which show you things Julie Tullis said and wrote. Note down any ideas you get about Julie's character and her love of climbing.
    e.g. 1 *She doesn't like to give up.*
2 An **autobiography** is a story of someone's life told by themselves. Write part of Julie's autobiography. Describe her feelings on the evening of 4 August when she reaches the summit. Include thoughts about the climb, reaching the summit, and the return journey. The photograph opposite will give you an idea of the route taken down K2.

K2: Julie's 'Mountain of mountains'. O = snowhole and X = camp 4 on the route down the mountain. There is less oxygen higher up the mountain. It gets harder to breathe and people cannot live long at great heights.

END OF UNIT REVIEW

1
2

Stay Safe

> **SKILLS YOU WILL USE IN THIS UNIT**
>
> **1** Giving your opinion in discussion and writing
>
> **2** Writing clear instructions
>
> **3** Conducting a survey and summarizing results
>
> **4** Reading for information
>
> **5** Writing a newspaper article

Accidents Happen

A An eight year-old Birmingham boy who tried to copy his father's method of killing weeds by pouring petrol onto them and setting the area alight, was burned when flashback caught his face and hair.

B A Birmingham mother who took her three month-old daughter to bed with her to keep warm, because she found the cost of central heating too much, accidentally smothered the child.

C A teenager, died when he was shot in the stomach at point blank range. The youth's uncle was carrying a shotgun which went off as he climbed a hedge near Monmouth.

D Two police officers brought a toddler back from the dead when he was pulled from a goldfish pond in his grandparents' back garden. There were no signs of life when the 23 month-old boy was rescued but the Berkshire police officers gave him the kiss of life.

E A baby was critically injured when the tip of a lighted cigarette dropped into the cot and set the bedding alight.

F A two year-old Staffordshire boy left 'for just a few minutes' while his mother fetched his nightclothes, drowned in his bathwater.

G Firemen had to break into a Smethwick house when twin brothers aged only 18 months locked their mother out in the garden. Flames leapt from the cooker grill as food the mother had been preparing caught fire and filled the kitchen with smoke.

H A makeshift bed warmer which a pensioner rigged up to save her heating bills burned down her bungalow home. The 85 year-old Bristol woman had put an electric iron inside a saucepan to keep her bed cosy and collapsed from exhaustion while fighting the blaze the contraption caused.

(from *ROSPA booklet*)

Dean's Lucky Escape

DEAN'S LIFE LINE!

FOUR-YEAR-OLD Dean Morrison is one of the luckiest boys around... because he owes his life to a clothes-line.

Dean escaped almost unscathed when he fell 80ft from the window of a fourth-floor flat.

And it was a rotary clothes-drier that broke his fall.

After a night in hospital for checks, Dean was back home yesterday playing happily with his toys and nursing only a few bruises.

The drama happened as Dean and his mother, Diane Jones, 22, were visiting a friend in Stockbridge, Edinburgh.

Mrs Jones, still shaken, said yesterday: 'I'm so relieved.

'The doctors were amazed. They could not believe he fell that far and survived with just a few bruises.'

The Mail on Sunday 28 June 1992

The path of Dean's fall on to the clothes-line.

What to do

In pairs

1 How far did Dean fall?
2 What saved his life?
3 How long did Dean stay in hospital?
4 What sort of injuries did he have?
5 How do you think his mother felt about the accident?
6 What could be done to prevent this sort of accident?

What to do next

On your own

Collect 2 or 3 accident report stories from your local newspaper. Cut them out and stick them into your book.

Write a few sentences about each report, saying who might have been to blame, and how the accident might have been prevented.

Firework Code

What to do

In pairs

Use these key words and phrases to help you to write a firework safety code.

carefully	distance	adults	safe	throw
indoors	children	never	closed box	torch
matches	pockets	instructions	pets	

Your code should have 6 to 8 rules. Write these in clear sentences so that young children can read and understand them.

What to do next

On your own

Ask 8 to 10 people in your group or class if they agree or disagree with this statement:

'Fireworks should not be sold to the general public. They should only be sold to people who put on organized displays.'

Record what they say in a table like this:

Name	Agree	Disagree	Reason
Sanjit	✓		People get hurt every year

Use your table to help you to write a public information leaflet with the title 'Should Fireworks be Banned?'.

Mountain Rescue

Mountain Rescue Post No. 34, Settle and sub-post, Malham
Cave Rescue Organisation,
Clapham, Lancaster LA2 8HH

Incidents 1990

April
9   Sunday 15th (18.25) MALHAM COVE – Walker (f, 65) slipped on wet, muddy grass above Cove. Badly sprained ankle. Inadequate footwear. Fell/N. Yorks.
10   Saturday 21st (15.15) WHERNSIDE– Entrant (m, 23) in Three Peaks charity event reported to have fractured leg in slip near summit. In fact, it was badly twisted and he had hobbled to the Hill Inn. Fell/N. Yorks.
11   (same day) (16.15) A65 Road, NEWBY – Assist at road traffic accident on returning from previous incident. Two people slightly injured when their car overturned. Other/N. Yorks.

June
20   Sunday 17th (11.45) FLUTED HOLE – Lamb rescued from bottom of 18m shaft.   Animal/N. Yorks.
21   Wednesday 27th (19.40) SHAFT BY WADE'S ENTRANCE – Lamb rescued from bottom of 6m deep rift.   Animal/N. Yorks.
22   Friday 29th (19. 00) SELL GILL HOLE – Sheep rescued from bottom of first pitch. Animal/N. Yorks
23   Saturday 30th (17.45) OLD ING CAVE – Seven cavers (two groups) trapped up Rough Hill Inlet by rapid flooding. Brought through 3m of flooded passage by cave divers and escorted out. Teams: CRO and Cave Diving Group.   Cave, inc. diving/N. Yorks.

December
39   Saturday 1st (19. 5) KINGSDALE MASTER CAVE – Caver (m, 23) fell while climbing pitch from streamway, unroped. Fractured wrist/arm. Cave/N. Yorks.
40   Saturday 8th (14.55) A65 Road East of HELLIFIELD – At Police request, check that cars abandonned in snow were unoccupied. Several drivers assisted by digging out their cars and lorries from metre-deep snow drifts. One lorry driver brought back to Settle. Other/N. Yorks.
41   Monday 24th (12.50) LANGCLIFFE – Assist Police in search for man (74), missing from son's house. Found by Police dog in neighbour's garden. Other/N. Yorks.
42   Saturday 29th (11.20) MEALBANK QUARRY, INGLETON – large sheep rescued from ledge.   Animal/N. Yorks.

On page 48 are some extracts from a report made by the cave rescue team based at Clapham, near Lancaster.

How to read the entries:

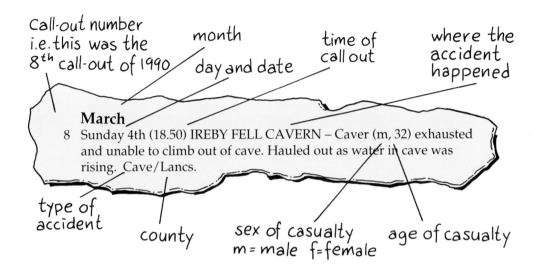

Call-out number i.e. this was the 8th call-out of 1990

month

day and date

time of call out

where the accident happened

March

8   Sunday 4th (18.50) IREBY FELL CAVERN – Caver (m, 32) exhausted and unable to climb out of cave. Hauled out as water in cave was rising. Cave/Lancs.

type of accident

county

sex of casualty m = male f = female

age of casualty

What to do

In a small group

1   Look at each call-out entry and say why the rescue team was called out.
    Could the accident have been avoided? If so, how?
2   Agree on which you think was the most serious incident. Give reasons.

What to do next

On your own

Pick one of the call-out entries and make up a short newspaper report about the incident.
  If you pick one of the animal rescues you might write about this in a light-hearted way using a headline such as: 'Crazy Sheep Goes Caving!'
  If you are writing about a human casualty the tone will of course be serious.

END OF UNIT REVIEW

1

2

Romeo and Juliet

SKILLS YOU WILL USE IN THIS UNIT

1 Reading a playscript

2 Discussing details of plot and character

3 Writing a diary entry

4 Comparing modern English with Shakespeare's English

About the Play

William Shakespeare was born in Stratford-upon-Avon in 1564. He wrote 37 plays including *Romeo and Juliet*.

Romeo and Juliet is a play about two young people (Juliet is only 13 years old, Romeo is 16) who fall in love. The play is set in fifteenth-century Italy. Juliet is a Capulet and Romeo a Montague. But these two powerful families are bitter enemies and their marriage would never be approved. They are married secretly and then Juliet's father says she will be made to marry Count Paris. In the end Romeo and Juliet's tragic deaths bring the two warring families together at last.

Prologue to the Play

This is the Prologue (a short introduction) from *Romeo and Juliet*:

Two households, both alike in dignity,
　In fair Verona, where we lay our scene,
From ancient grudge break to new mutiny,
　Where civil blood makes civil hands unclean.
From forth the fatal loins of these two foes
　A pair of star-cross'd lovers take their life;
Whose misadventur'd piteous overthrows
　Doth with their death bury their parents' strife.
The fearful passage of their death-mark'd love,
　And the continuance of their parents' rage,
Which, but their children's end, nought could remove,
　Is now the two hours' traffic of our stage;
The which if you with patient ears attend,
What here shall miss, our toil shall strive to mend.

(from *Act 1 Scene 1*)

What to do

In a small group

1 Write down the words and phrases in the Prologue which tell you these things:
   A where the play takes place
   B how long the play lasts
   C that the two families are both powerful
   D that the argument between them has been going on for a long time
   E that Romeo and Juliet die
   F that the death of Romeo and Juliet brings their families together
2 Why does Shakespeare describe Romeo and Juliet as a pair of star-crossed lovers?

The Plot Thickens

In this scene Juliet's mother (Lady Capulet) tells her daughter that she must marry County Paris. Juliet is already secretly married to Romeo. Also present are Juliet's father (Capulet) and her servant (Nurse).

Lady Capulet: Marry, my child, early next Thursday morn
The gallant, young, and noble gentleman,
The County Paris, at Saint Peter's church,
Shall happily make thee there a joyful bride.

Juliet: Now, by Saint Peter's church, and Peter too,
He shall not make me there a joyful bride!
I wonder at this haste; that I must wed
Ere he that should be husband comes to woo.
I pray you, tell my lord and father, madam,
I will not marry yet; and, when I do, I swear,
It shall be Romeo, whom you know I hate,
Rather than Paris. These are news indeed!

Lady Capulet: Here comes your father; tell him so yourself,
And see how he will take it at your hands.

(*Enter Capulet and Nurse*)

Capulet: When the sun sets, the air doth drizzle dew;
But for the sunset of my brother's son
It rains downright.
How now! A conduit girl? What, still in tears?
Evermore showering? In one little body
Thou counterfeit'st a bark, a sea, a wind;
For still thy eyes, which I may call the sea,
Do ebb and flow with tears; the bark thy body is,
Who, raging with thy tears, and they with them,
Without a sudden calm, will overset
Thy tempest-tossed body. How now, wife?
Have you deliver'd to her our decree?

Lady Capulet: Ay, sir; but she will none, she gives you thanks.
I would the fool were married to her grave!

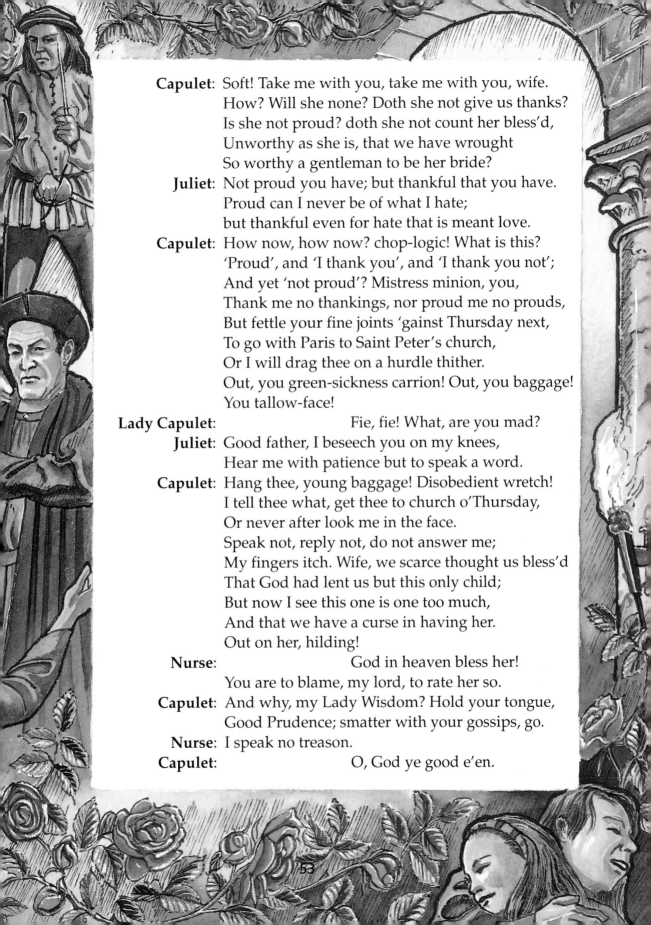

Capulet: Soft! Take me with you, take me with you, wife.
How? Will she none? Doth she not give us thanks?
Is she not proud? doth she not count her bless'd,
Unworthy as she is, that we have wrought
So worthy a gentleman to be her bride?

Juliet: Not proud you have; but thankful that you have.
Proud can I never be of what I hate;
but thankful even for hate that is meant love.

Capulet: How now, how now? chop-logic! What is this?
'Proud', and 'I thank you', and 'I thank you not';
And yet 'not proud'? Mistress minion, you,
Thank me no thankings, nor proud me no prouds,
But fettle your fine joints 'gainst Thursday next,
To go with Paris to Saint Peter's church,
Or I will drag thee on a hurdle thither.
Out, you green-sickness carrion! Out, you baggage!
You tallow-face!

Lady Capulet: Fie, fie! What, are you mad?

Juliet: Good father, I beseech you on my knees,
Hear me with patience but to speak a word.

Capulet: Hang thee, young baggage! Disobedient wretch!
I tell thee what, get thee to church o'Thursday,
Or never after look me in the face.
Speak not, reply not, do not answer me;
My fingers itch. Wife, we scarce thought us bless'd
That God had lent us but this only child;
But now I see this one is one too much,
And that we have a curse in having her.
Out on her, hilding!

Nurse: God in heaven bless her!
You are to blame, my lord, to rate her so.

Capulet: And why, my Lady Wisdom? Hold your tongue,
Good Prudence; smatter with your gossips, go.

Nurse: I speak no treason.

Capulet: O, God ye good e'en.

Nurse: May not one speak?

Capulet: Peace, you mumbling fool!
Utter your gravity o'er a gossip's bowl;
For here we need it not.

Lady Capulet: You are too hot.

Capulet: God's bread! It makes me mad.
Day, night, hour, tide, time, work, play,
Alone, in company – still my care hath been
To have her match'd. And having now provided
A gentleman of noble parentage,
Of fair demesnes, youthful, and nobly lin'd
Stuff'd, as they say, with honourable parts,
Proportion'd as one's thought would wish a man—
And then to have a wretched puling fool,
A whining mammet, in her fortune's tender,
To answer 'I'll not wed, I cannot love,
I am too young, I pray you pardon me'.
But, and you will not wed, I'll pardon you:
Graze where you will, you shall not house with me.
Look to 't, think on 't; I do not use to jest.
Thursday is near. Lay hand on heart; advise.
And you be mine, I'll give you to my friend;
And you be not, hang, beg, starve, die in the streets,
For, by my soul, I'll ne'er ackowledge thee,
Nor what is mine shall never do thee good.
Trust to 't, bethink you. I'll not be forsworn.

(*Exit*)

Juliet: Is there no pity sitting in the clouds,
That sees into the bottom of my grief?
O sweet my mother, cast me not away!
Delay this marriage for a month, a week;
Or, if you do not, make the marriage bed
In that dim monument where Tybalt lies.

Lady Capulet: Talk not to me, for I'll not speak a word.
Do as thou wilt, for I have done with thee.

(*Exit*)

(from *Act 3 Scene 5*)

In pairs

1 When and where is the wedding to take place?
2 How does Juliet feel about the wedding?
3 How does Juliet's father react and why?
4 What do you think about her father's reaction?
5 What does Juliet mean when she says she will 'make the marriage bed in that dim monument where Tybalt lies'?
6 What do you think Juliet will do after her mother refuses to help her?

What to do next

On your own

Juliet shows a great strength of character when she rebels against her father's plans
    Write her diary entry, describing her feelings about their argument. Include details of her possible plans for the future.

The language of the play

What to do

In a small group

1 Some of the language in the play is quite like everyday speech today:
      e.g.   *'I will not marry yet; and, when I do.........'*
But most of the play reads like poetry:
      e.g.   *'Is there no pity sitting in the clouds,*
             That sees into the bottom of my grief?'
Find 2 more examples in the extract where the language is more poetic.
2 The extracts contain a number of words or phrases that are not used in everyday speech today.
      e.g.   *'How now?'* and *'Out, you baggage!'*
See if you can find other words and phrases like this. Try to find out what they mean.

END OF UNIT REVIEW

1
2

Unit 9

Are You Persuaded?

SKILLS YOU WILL USE IN THIS UNIT

1 Conducting research on adverts

2 Presenting arguments in a role play

3 Discussing attitudes in adverts

4 Discussing design techniques used in adverts

5 Looking at persuasive language

6 Writing and designing an advert

Advertising All Around

What to do

On your own

1 Explain in one sentence the point which this illustration is making about young people and advertising.

2 Make a note of all the adverts you see or hear in one day. These might be on TV, in magazines, or in shop windows, for example. Record your findings under these headings:

Monday 19. Oct.   7.40 am - 10.00 pm
Researching adverts seen/heard today

TV	Newspapers	Billboards	Radio	Magazines	Shops
IIII	II	III	IIII	IIII|	IIII|

3 Compare you results with others in your group.

4 Describe the advert you remember best from the whole day. What makes it so memorable?

What to do next

In pairs

1 Look up the verb 'to persuade' in a dictionary.

2 Use a thesaurus to list verbs which mean the same or a similar thing.

3 Role play with your partner a situation in which you might persuade or be persuaded to do a certain thing.
e.g. Your friend tries to persuade you to do the washing up.

4 Listen carefully to the role play prepared by another pair. List any persuasive words or phrases they use. Perform your role play for them and then compare your lists of words.

Special Offers

What to do

In pairs

Study the 3 adverts on this page. Then say whether the following statements are true (T), false (F), or if there is not enough evidence (NEE).

A All the adverts are aimed at people below the age of 20.

B Two of the adverts contain offers of another product.

C One of the offers will cost extra money.

D The price of each product is made clear in each advert.

E None of the adverts are sexist.

F One of the adverts sells a very exciting product.

G All the adverts use cartoons to appeal to young people.

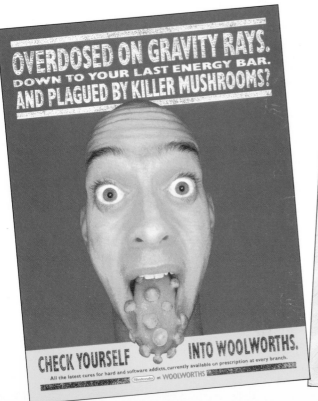

In a small group

1 Make a note of any words or phrases used in the adverts which you think may have been invented or given a new meaning in the past 50 years, e.g. software.

2 List any words you and your friends use when you 'rave' about something.

3 Note down any words on your list which people may find hard to understand in 50 years' time.

4 Write an advert for a new fizzy drink or snack to appear in a pop magazine. Use some of the words from your list to appeal to people of your age.

Look at the labels on the advert below for milk. Try to include a catchy product name, a slogan, an eye-catching picture and a short description of the product in your advert.

Slogan with catchy rhyme

Lettering large and in bold

Repeated 't' sounds to emphasize rhyme

Word 'bottle' has double meaning

Dramatic image

Features young, attractive, and healthy person

Product appears twice in the picture

Ancient Adverts

2

This beautiful trick is simply (to all appearance) a fancy finger-ring, silver-plated, and being of an odd pattern, immediately arrests the attention of any friend, who will naturally ask to examine it. Attached to this ring is a small rubber ball, which is held in the palm of the hand, so as to prevent detection. This ball is filled with water, and when a person examines it that you wish to play the trick on, you have only to close your hand, which will throw a small steady stream of water directly in a person's face. Once filling the ball is sufficient to operate the trick one dozen times.

The Finger-Ring Trick.
SOMETHING NEW AND RICH.

1

Bailey's Swimming Glove.
LIKE A DUCK'S FOOT.

Pat applied for

Learn to swim, to float, to become in water as expert as a DUCK by using Bailey's Rubber Swimming Glove. They are made of Pure Rubber, which makes a web between the fingers like a duck's foot, doubling the power of the stroke, and greatly increasing the speed, ease, and pleasure of swimming.

Men's $2;
Women's, $1.75;
Children's, $1.50 Pair.
Sent postage paid on receipt of price.

3

WANTED! 100,000 BOYS

TO SEND FOR THE CANDY STORE

THE BOSS CANDY STORE

BRANCH OF MITCHELL & WHITELAW'S CINCINNATI CANDY FACTORY

JAW BREAKERS	BULLS EYES	ARABIAN GUM STORE
SUGAR CURED HAMS	PEERLESS BUTTER SCOTCH	CREEK FIG PASTE
ASSORTED STICK CANDY	LONG NINE MOLASSES CANDY STICKS	
RUBBER CHEWING GUM	CREAM CHOCOLATE DROPS	

STORE OPEN

Active, intelligent Boys, who can count money, are making from 50 cents to $1.00 per day, after school, at home, among their playmates. Each one a complete Store, with large sign, circulars to distribute, etc., and over 450 articles of Fancy Candies, to retail at one cent each. Money doubled in a few days. 'It's lots of fun.' Sent by express on receipt of $2.00; full description and list of articles sent on receipt of three-cent stamp.

4

Do You Chew Gum?

Here is a little novelty every one who loves to chew gum will appreciate. 'Peggy' is its name. 'Peggy' is a convenient and handsomely decorated tin box with a peg in the center to hold your gum when not in use. 'Peggy' keeps the gum clean, cool, healthful and handy. 'Peggy' can be carried in the pocket, satchel or attached to cord or chain. The more 'Peggy' is used the better it is liked. Mailed postpaid on receipt of 5 cents. Agents wanted.

What to do

In a small group

1 Each phrase given on page 61 has been taken from one of the original adverts above. Match the persuasive phrases A–L to the products 1–4. Write your answers like this.

   e.g. D = 3

2 Make up a snappy slogan advertising any 2 of these products.

   e.g. Product 4 = Chew now, chew later!

A   something new and rich

B   clean, cool, healthful, and handy

C   everyone who loves...

D   Wanted! 100,000 Boys   E   send for...

F   greatly increasing the speed, ease and pleasure

G   money doubled in a few days

H   the more it is used, the better it is liked

I   active, intelligent Boys

J   this beautiful trick

K   arrests the attention of any friend

L   lots of fun

What to do next

In pairs
1 Look back at the adverts on page 60 and pick the one you
both find the most interesting. Make notes on the way the
advert is designed. Include ideas about:
  ● the use of illustration
  ● who the product is aimed at
  ● the language used (which words sound old fashioned
    and which sound more familiar?)
  ● examples of sexism
  ● other ways the adverts are different from modern
    adverts
Share you ideas on this advert with the rest of your group.

Adverts Old and New

1951 Mercury

Streaking over the open road the **1951 MERCURY** gives you real excitement

The new 1951 Mercury Convertible is sleek, massive, low to the road
—with clean, flowing lines accented by gleaming new trim.
The newly developed speed-style rear fenders . . . contoured
bumper following rear body lines . . . give custom-styled appearance.

1934 Lanchester

No. L.47.

The New "18" **Lanchester**

with the wonderful
DAIMLER
FLUID·FLYWHEEL
SELF-CHANGING
TRANSMISSION

Saloons from
£595

1958 Wolseley

Buy wisely — buy
WOLSELEY

For a compact car with
exceptional motoring quali-
ties the Fifteen Hundred is
an obvious choice. High-speed cruising
in top makes driving over long dis-
tances effortless, while the high third
gear ensures brisk acceleration when
overtaking. Note the attractive interior,
distinctively upholstered in traditional
Wolseley style and featuring the beautiful grained walnut fascia panel. Duotone
body finishes at extra cost.

The FIFTEEN HUNDRED

1974 Jaguar

XJ6C All the refinements and performance of the XJ6
in an elegant new full-four seat two-door coupé

62

1993 Rover

THE ROVER 214i. THE EXCITEMENT IS UNREAL.
(THE PRICE IS UNEXPECTED.)

200 SERIES
ABOVE ALL, WE'RE ROVER DEALERS

What to do

On your own

1 Create an appealing advert for one of these products:
- a car
- a mountain bike
- a new perfume

Your advert will appear in a TV magazine which is read by adults. Decide on your product name, make up a slogan for it, and choose a picture that will 'sell' it. Remember to write a brief description of your product using persuasive language.

2 Choose any product advertised in this week's magazines. Design an advert for this product that could have appeared in a newspaper in 1880.
Decide how the product would be illustrated. Use suitable words and phrases from the old ads in this unit to help you describe the product.

3 Imagine that you are in a busy shopping centre when you are approached by a space traveller. The traveller is very confused by the advertising all around.
Write the explanation you would give the traveller to help her/him understand advertising. Include:
- a definition of the word 'advert' (You could compare your ideas with a dictionary definition.)
- an explanation of the techniques used by advertisers. The illustration on page 56 and the advert on page 59 will help you decide what to write.

END OF UNIT REVIEW

1
2

Oxford University Press, Walton Street, Oxford OX2 6DP

Oxford New York
Athens Auckland Bangkok Bombay
Calcutta Cape Town Dar es Salaam Delhi
Florence Hong Kong Istanbul Karachi
Kuala Lumpur Madras Madrid Melbourne
Mexico City Nairobi Paris Singapore
Taipei Tokyo Toronto

and associated companies in
Berlin Ibadan

Oxford is a trade mark of Oxford University Press

© Selection and Activities Chris Culshaw and Jill Dodgson 1994
First published by Oxford University Press 1994
Reprinted 1995

ISBN 0 19 831432 9

Cover illustration by Alan Nanson

Printed in Hong Kong

In the same series:

Headwork Book 1	0 19 833372 2
Headwork Book 2	0 19 833373 0
Headwork Book 3	0 19 833374 9
Headwork Book 4	0 19 833375 7
Headwork Book 5	0 19 833387 0
Headwork Book 6	0 19 833388 9
Headwork Book 7	0 19 833389 7
Headwork Book 8	0 19 833390 0
English Headwork Book 1	0 19 833376 5
English Headwork Book 2	0 19 833377 3
English Headwork Book 3	0 19 833378 1
English Headwork Book 4	0 19 833379 X
Headwork Stories Book 1	0 19 833380 3
Headwork Stories Book 2	0 19 833381 1
Headwork Stories Book 3	0 19 833391 9
Headwork Stories Book 4	0 19 833392 7
Headwork Anthologies Book 1	0 19 833396 X
Headwork Anthologies Book 2	0 19 833397 8
Headwork Anthologies Book 3	0 19 833398 6